Celebrating Islamic FESTIVALS

LIZ MILES

raintree

a Capstone company — publishers for children

Raintree is an imprint of Capstone Global Library Limited, a company incorporated in England and Wales having its registered office at 7 Pilgrim Street, London, EC4V 6LB – Registered company number: 6695582

www.raintree.co.uk
myorders@raintree.co.uk

Edited by James Benefield
Designed by Steve Mead
Original illustrations © Capstone Global Library Limited
Picture research by Eric Gohl
Production by Helen McCreath
Originated by Capstone Global Library Limited
Printed and bound in China

ISBN 978 1 406 29767 6
19 18 17 16 15
10 9 8 7 6 5 4 3 2 1

British Library Cataloguing in Publication Data
A full catalogue record for this book is available from the British Library.

Acknowledgements
Alamy: See Li, 39; AP Photo: Amel Emric, 8, Murad Sezer, 23; Bridgeman Images: Archives Charmet/Private Collection, 20; Capstone Studio: Karon Dubke, 14–15 (all), 26–27 (all), 32–33 (all); Corbis: Demotix/Antoni Halim, 38, Demotix/rudianto, 42 (bottom); Courtesy of Mawlid in the City: 16; Dreamstime: Feroze, 40, Zurijeta, 34; Getty Images: AFP/Stringer, 7, Dan Kitwood, 30, Greg Elms, 37, Leemage, 11, Stringer/Arif Ali, 19, Stringer/Nikolay Doychinov, 42 (middle), Stringer/Jaafar Ashtiyeh, cover, Stringer/Kevin Frayer, 31; iStockphoto: KailashSoni, 42 (top); Newscom: EPA/Abed Al Hashlamoun, 18, 21, EPA/Khaled El-Fiqi, 43 (middle), Hindustan Times, 24, NOTIMEX/Saeed Ahmad, 29, Pakistan Press International Photo, 25, Universal Images Group/Leemage, 12, Xinhua News Agency/Chong Voon Chung, 36, ZUMA Press/Ashraf Amra, 35, ZUMA Press/Issam Rimawi, 28, ZUMA Press/Julie Edwards, 10; Shutterstock: artpixelgraphy image, 17, hikrcn, 9, khazari, 43 (top), Ulysses_ua, 13, ZouZou, 41, Zurijeta, 43 (bottom); Wikimedia: B. Simpson, 22.

Design Elements: Shutterstock

SAFETY TIPS FOR THE RECIPES
Trying new recipes is fun, but before you start working in the kitchen, keep these safety tips in mind:
- Always ask an adult for permission, especially when using the hob, oven or sharp knives.
- At the hob, always point saucepan handles away from the edge. Don't keep flammable materials, such as towels, too close to the burners. Have a fire extinguisher nearby. Don't lean too close when you lift a lid off a pan – steam can cause burns, too. Always use oven gloves when taking dishes out of the oven.
- Wash your hands before you work, and wash your workspace and utensils after you are done. Cook foods completely. Don't use expired or spoiled food. Be careful when you cut with knives.
- Work with an adult – together you can both learn about religions of the world through food!

Contents

What is Islam? 4

Islamic New Year..8

Why is the Prophet's birthday important?....... 16

Miraj...20

Ramadan.. 22

Celebrating the Hajj......................................34

Family celebrations 38

Celebrations around the world.......................42

Cookery tips 44

Timeline..45

Glossary 46

Find out more..47

Index 48

Some words are shown in bold, **like this**. You can find out what they mean by looking in the glossary.

WHAT IS ISLAM?

Islam is the second biggest religion in the world. It has over a billion followers, called Muslims.

Muslims believe in one God, called Allah, and follow the **Prophet** Muhammad (pbuh, see page 5). They believe that people should live according to the will of Allah. If they disobey Allah, they can ask for forgiveness and Allah will pardon them. Everyone will finally be judged and sent to heaven or hell.

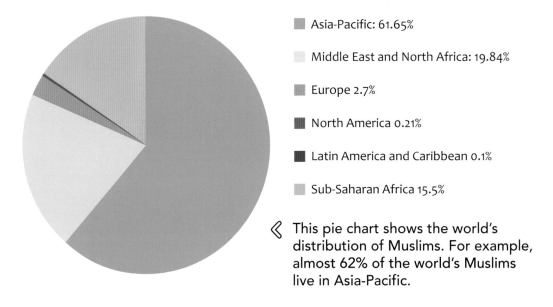

- Asia-Pacific: 61.65%
- Middle East and North Africa: 19.84%
- Europe 2.7%
- North America 0.21%
- Latin America and Caribbean 0.1%
- Sub-Saharan Africa 15.5%

≪ This pie chart shows the world's distribution of Muslims. For example, almost 62% of the world's Muslims live in Asia-Pacific.

Who is the Prophet Muhammad?

In Arabia, in 610 CE, Muhammad heard the voice of an angel saying that Allah had chosen him as a Prophet. He heard words from Allah throughout his life. The words were later written down as the Qur'an.

Muhammad believed in one God. People in his home town of Mecca (also known as Makkah) did not like this, as they believed in more than one god. In 622 CE, Muhammad moved to Medina, where the first Islamic community grew. By the time Muhammad died in 632 CE, he had moved back to Mecca, with most of Arabia becoming Islamic.

⌃ This map shows some places that are important to Muslims and the history of Islam.

What does "pbuh" mean?

Muhammad and other prophets mentioned in the Qur'an, such as Noah, **Abraham, Moses** and **Jesus**, are so well respected that "peace be upon him" is said after their names are mentioned. Sometimes it is written in an abbreviated form: pbuh. Also, the names Muslims use for these figures are Ibrahim (Abraham), Musa (Moses) and Isa (Jesus).

Holy books

The Qur'an helps Muslims to understand Allah and know how to live. The book is treated with respect. When people read it aloud, everyone must be quiet. Many Muslims learn it by heart. The Qur'an is written in Arabic, so Muslim children all around the world start to learn to read Arabic from an early age.

The Hadith is also important. It is a collection of reports on what Muhammad and his followers said and did.

How do Muslims celebrate their festivals?

Islamic festivals are celebrated by Muslims all over the world. Many festivals mark events in the history of Islam and the life of Muhammad. For example, the festival of Laylat al-Qadr (the Night of Power) celebrates the night Muhammad first heard words from Allah.

Fasts and feasts

Festivals are busy and friendly times, but can also be times of quiet prayers. Cards and gifts are often exchanged, and crowds gather at mosques for prayers.

Feasts and **fasts** are both important. Traditional foods are prepared. Families and friends gather in their homes to share meals. Fasting is especially important during the holy month of Ramadan.

The Five Pillars of Islam

According to the Hadith, Muhammad taught five important principles to help Muslims in their faith. They are called the Five Pillars of Islam, listed here with their basic meanings.

1. Declaration of Faith (Shahadah) – to declare publicly a belief that "There is no God but Allah and Muhammad is His Messenger"
2. Prayer (Salah) – to pray five times a day
3. Charity (Zakah) – to give a part of his or her wealth to help the poor
4. Fasting (Sawm) – to not eat or drink during daylight hours during Ramadan (see pages 22–33)
5. **Pilgrimage** (Hajj) – to go on a pilgrimage to Mecca at least once in a Muslim's life (see pages 34–35)

△ Muslims celebrate the Islamic New Year all around the world. These students, dressed in traditional costume, are taking part in a parade in Indonesia, home to more than 200 million Muslims.

ISLAMIC NEW YEAR

The first month of the year on the Islamic calendar is called Muharram. The first day of Muharram is New Year's Day, called Al Hijra. Rather than a major holiday, it's a time for thoughtful, quiet celebration.

Muslims make New Year resolutions to decide on how they can live better lives through the year ahead. Stories about the Prophet Muhammad are told, especially the Hijra: Muhammad's journey to Medina.

After Hijra

The New Year is called Al Hijra because Muhammad's Hijra (journey) in 622 CE led to the setting up of the first Islamic community. The Islamic calendar (see the page opposite) begins with the date of Muhammad's Hijra, too. A.H. – which means After Hijra – is sometimes written after Islamic dates.

⌃ A Muslim saying her prayers for New Year at a mosque in Sarajevo, in Bosnia and Herzegovina.

At New Year, Muslims celebrate how the Prophet Muhammad moved from his own **tribe** in Mecca and set up a **spiritual** community in Medina. This showed how living in a community bound by shared beliefs in Allah, and obedience to Allah, was more important than staying with a person's own tribe or family. The community's values and way of living became the basis of Islamic life.

⌃ Today, millions of Muslims visit the tomb of Muhammad in Medina.

LUNAR CALENDAR

The Islamic Hijra calendar follows the Moon's cycle. There are 12 months in the year; each monthstarts with the new moon. This calendar is about 11 days shorter than the 365-day Gregorian calendar, which follows the Sun's cycle. Most people in the West (such as the United Kingdom and the United States) follow the Gregorian calendar.

Islamic Calendar

1 **Muharram**
   1 Al Hijra (New Year's Day)
   10 Ashura
2 **Safar**
3 **Rabi' al-awwal**
   12 (Sunni) Mawlid an-Nabi (Birth of Muhammad)
   17 (Shi'a) Mawlid an-Nabi (Birth of Muhammad)
4 **Rabi' al-thani**
5 **Jumada al-awwal**
6 **Jumada al-thani**
7 **Rajab**
   27 Laylat al-Miraj (Night of Ascension)
8 **Sha'ban**
9 **Ramadan**
   27 Laylat al-Qadr (Night of Power)
10 **Shawwal**
   1 Id al-Fitr (Feast of Breaking the Fast)
11 **Dhu al-Qi'dah**
12 **Dhu al-Hijjah**
   10 Id al-Adha (Feast of Sacrifice)

Who celebrates Ashura?

Sunni and Shi'a are the two main groups of Islam. Sunnis are the majority, making up about 85 per cent of Muslims. Shi'a Muslims mark the 10th day of Muharram, called Ashura, as a day of mourning for Hussein – the Prophet's grandson – who died for his beliefs.

Now & Then

Day of Mourning

Some Shi'a Muslims have made themselves suffer in memory of Hussein's death, for example by whipping their bodies with chains. However, Shi'a leaders now discourage this **ritual**. Instead, people are told to donate their blood to medical charities, to help others in need.

Case study

THE ASHURA PROCESSION, LONDON

Up to 3,000 men, women and children from different backgrounds gather for Ashura in London every year. Shi'a Muslims hold a procession through the streets and give speeches at Marble Arch. Mourning Hussein, they wear black, beat their chests with their hand and chant.

Sunnis and Shi'as

Sunni and Shi'a Muslims share the same basic beliefs, but they first split after the Prophet Muhammad died. Abu Bakr was the first elected leader, or **caliph**, of the Muslims. But the Shi'as believe that the successor should have been Alī ibn Abī Tālib, the Prophet's cousin and son-in-law.

Alī ibn Abī Tālib was married to Fatima, one of the Prophet's daughters. Shi'a is short for Shi'at Ali (the Party of Ali), and Alī became the fourth caliph.

Shi'as continued to believe that the caliph should always be descended from Alī and Fatima. Sunnis believed in a system of election instead. Alī and his son Hussein were assassinated in a battle for power while fighting at Karbala in 680 CE. This led to the Shi'as' focus on the importance of **martyrdom** and mourning, a belief which is still followed today.

≫ A miniature illustration from a historical Turkish manuscript. Here, Abu Bakr (in red, on the left) is recognized as the first leader of the Muslims. People and animals are not often shown in Islamic art. This is because some Muslims see these representations as **graven images**.

11

Noah's ark

In Islamic teachings, Noah tried to get people to worship the one God, Allah, instead of many gods and stone **idols**, but the people refused. Allah inspired Noah, a skilled carpenter, to make an ark, load it with animals and his family.

∧ This miniature Turkish Islamic 16th-century painting illustrates the story of Noah in his ark, and the rains sent by Allah to flood the Earth.

Allah then caused rains to flood the land, so all the unbelievers drowned, including Noah's son. The rains eventually stopped and the Day of Ashura marks the time when the ark finally rested on dry land.

Noah's pudding

It is said that when Noah's ark came to rest after the flood, Noah's family celebrated with a special dish. They used the few ingredients they had available, such as dried fruits and grains, to make a pudding.

Many Sunni Muslims fast on Ashura, but there is no law saying they must. Some end this fast with a special pudding called ashure or Noah's pudding, in memory of Noah (see pages 14–15 for the recipe).

Moses and the Red Sea

Ashura is also recorded as the day the Prophet Moses and his followers were saved by Allah. Moses's mission was to lead his followers (who believed in one God) to safety, away from the cruel Egyptian **pharaoh** and his army.

Moses and his people reached the Red Sea and Allah opened a path up in the waters for them to escape. The path then closed and the Egyptian soldiers who followed were drowned.

⌃ An aerial photo showing the Red Sea, which lies between Africa and Asia.

Noah's
Pudding

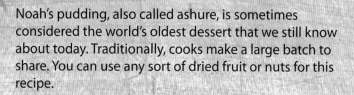

TIME:

Overnight (about 8 hours) plus 1½ hours

SERVES:

8 to 10 people

TOOLS:

large saucepan, with lid
weighing scales
strainer
stirring spoon
knife and cutting board
grater with small holes or a zester
ladle

Vegetarian

Vegan

Dairy Free

Noah's pudding, also called ashure, is sometimes considered the world's oldest dessert that we still know about today. Traditionally, cooks make a large batch to share. You can use any sort of dried fruit or nuts for this recipe.

INGREDIENTS:

220 g dried barley
water
1 drained can of cannellini beans, rinsed
1 drained can of chickpeas (also called garbanzo beans), rinsed
12 dried apricots, diced
60 g raisins
zest of an orange (about 1 tablespoon)
360 g white sugar
cinnamon, crushed walnuts, pomegranate seeds for garnish

STEPS:

Put the barley in the large saucepan. Add water to about 3 cm above the barley. Cover and let the barley soak overnight. By the next day, the barley will have soaked up a lot of the water.

2 Drain the barley of excess water, and return to the pot. Add 2 l of fresh water, bring to a boil and then cover and reduce the heat to low. Let it simmer for 30 minutes until the barley is creamy, and has soaked up most of the liquid.

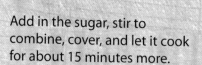 Add the beans, chickpeas, apricots, raisins, orange zest and another 1 litre of water. Stir to combine. Bring to a boil, and then cover and reduce the heat to low. Let it simmer for about 45 minutes.

Add in the sugar, stir to combine, cover, and let it cook for about 15 minutes more. **4**

5 Serve your pudding hot or cold. Ladle it into bowls, sprinkle with cinnamon and garnish with the nuts and pomegranate seeds.

WHY IS THE PROPHET'S BIRTHDAY IMPORTANT?

Mawlid means "birthday", and Mawlid an-Nabi is the birthday of the Prophet Muhammad. It is on 12th day of the month Rabi' al-awwal, although Shi'a Muslims celebrate it five days later.

Mawlid is a big event and a national holiday in countries where the main religion is Islam. There can be street celebrations and processions. In countries where fewer Muslims live, it's a smaller event. There, it is often celebrated at home and in mosques.

However, a minority of Muslims do not approve of the celebrations. They think that it puts too much emphasis on a human prophet. Also, they point out how the Prophet never asked his followers to celebrate the day.

Case study

"MAWLID IN THE CITY"

A group of Muslims decided to run an international "Mawlid in the City" event each year in the UK. They wanted to share the teachings of Islam. They also wanted to show how they devote their lives to following the example of the Prophet Muhammad and Allah's teachings.

For the event, Muslims gave out roses, chocolates and greetings cards to people in the streets of cities such as London and Coventry. They explained Islamic values, such as peace, love and mercy.

The importance of the Prophet

Muhammad lived between 570–632 CE. His mother died when he was only six, and his father had died before he was born. His grandfather, and then his uncle, a merchant, looked after him. Muhammad travelled with his uncle, and he became a good businessman.

When he was 25, he married a widow called Khadija and had two sons, but both died in childhood. Muhammad was 40 when he heard the first words from Allah. It is thought that this happened while he was in a cave on Mount Hira, near Mecca.

⌃ Muslims gather to pray at the cave on Mount Hira, near Mecca in Saudi Arabia.

Mawlid in Islamic countries

In countries where Islam is the main religion, there are all kinds of celebrations for Mawlid an-Nabi. For example:

- mosques are decorated with lights
- tents are put up in streets for the performance of plays and songs
- the Qur'an is read and people gather to learn more about Muhammad's life and the teachings of the Qur'an
- special sweets are made for sharing, especially amongst the children.

⌃ These Palestinian children are reading the Qur'an – believed to be the words of Allah revealed to Muhammad.

The colour green

Green is the most important colour for Muslims. It is said to have been Muhammad's favourite colour and that he wore a green cloak and turban. In the Qur'an, paradise is described as a garden, a green oasis, or watering hole.

Case study

PAKISTAN

About 96 per cent of people in Pakistan are Muslims, and the Prophet's birthday is celebrated throughout Rabi' al-awwal. They call it the Prophet's Birth Month and the 12th is called Milad-un-Nabi (note the slight difference in spelling).

For Milad-un-Nabi, hundreds of thousands gather in a vast park in the city of Lahore to celebrate and listen to speeches. Throughout the country, songs are sung and poetry, called naat, is recited in honour of the Prophet. The national flag is raised on public buildings, and adults and children march through the streets, holding specially made green flags for Milad.

⌃ A man throwing rose petals as a mark of respect, over the Mawlid (Milad) procession in Lahore, Pakistan.

MIRAJ

Miraj is one of the most important dates on the Islamic calendar (27 Rajab). It marks the night when Muhammad was taken up to heaven and was told by Allah that all Muslims should pray five times a day. Another name for the celebration is Laylat al-Miraj.

The Miraj legend

While asleep one night, Prophet Muhammad's heart was **purified** and filled with wisdom by two angels. He then travelled on a winged horse-like creature from Mecca to Jerusalem. The journey is called Isra (night journey) and Miraj (ascent). There, he met the prophets Ibrahim, Musa and Isa before being in the presence of Allah.

⟱ Muhammad rode on a mythical creature called Buraq. The name comes from the Arabic word "Bar'q" which means "light" or "electricity". It suggests Buraq could travel as quickly as the speed of light, or a bolt of lightning.

Remembering the Prophet's journey

Some Muslims believe the Prophet's journey should not be celebrated. They point out that no one knows the actual date and that Muhammad did not tell his followers to celebrate it.

For those who do celebrate the event, they tell the story to children in the mosques. There are special prayers and readings from the Qur'an. Some people choose to fast.

It is a public holiday in Islamic countries. For example, in the United Arab Emirates, music and dance halls close out of respect, and many Muslims pray late into the night.

⌃ Islamic children like these Palestinians often study the Qur'an before the holiday of Miraj.

RAMADAN

Ramadan falls on the ninth month of the Islamic calendar. It is very important to Muslims, and a time for fasting during daylight hours. It is believed that during this month the word of Allah (the Qur'an) was first revealed to the Prophet Muhammad.

A holy month

Muslims must not eat or drink during the daylight hours of Ramadan. During Ramadan, Muslims also:

- try to give up bad habits and thoughts
- spend more time praying
- read the Qur'an more often
- go to the mosque for special services.

Why fast?

Fasting is a way of obeying Allah; it also helps Muslims to focus on Allah and learn self-discipline. It is a reminder of the pain felt by the poor and hungry, and the importance of charity.

⌃ This is a Ramadan lantern from Cairo, Egypt.

Now & Then

Memories

Older people remember traditions that have since disappeared. For example, someone used to go around the streets banging a drum and calling people's names to get them to wake for an early meal before a fast. Some people remember making traditional Ramadan lanterns by hand. Today, mass-produced lanterns are bought by many families.

Case study

RAMADAN AROUND THE WORLD

In Islamic countries like Morocco and Kuwait, nearly everyone fasts. Businesses and schools open earlier as everyone gets up early for a pre-dawn meal. They also close earlier so everyone can get home to prepare for a meal eaten at sunset. If you are spotted eating or drinking in daylight in Kuwait, you are fined. The number of daylight (fasting) hours varies around the world, depending on the place and time of year.

⌃ Traditional puppets are used to tell a different Islamic story in Turkey for each night of Ramadan.

Ramadan meals

During Ramadan, Muslims share special family meals. They get up before dawn for suhoor, a pre-dawn meal. After sunset, the family shares a larger meal called **Iftar**, which may include dishes such as the one appearing in the pages 26–27.

Suhoor

It is important to eat food that is quick to prepare early in the morning. The food has to be nutritious, too. This is because working Muslims need to have enough energy to get through the daylight hours without feeling faint. It is recorded that the Prophet Muhammad said that the best suhoor is dates, so they are a popular choice today.

⌃ An Indian family wait to begin their iftar after fasting all day.

Case study

FASTING DURING SPORTING EVENTS

Ramadan can sometimes occur at the same time as an important sports event, such as the Olympics. Muslim athletes have to decide whether to compete without daytime food or drinks. Many do fast, but others postpone it. Mo Farah, an Olympic gold champion, made the hard decision to make up the days of fasting after the Olympics.

Who need not fast?

Children under the age of about seven are not expected to fast, and older children do not fast for the whole month until they become teenagers. Others who do not have to fast include the elderly, travellers and people who should not fast for medical reasons.

Case study

Iftar in Pakistan

Across cities in Pakistan, a siren sounds and there is a call to prayer from the mosques. After prayers, everyone celebrates. Many people go out to buy Iftar food from roadside stalls, to celebrate the end of the day's fast. Iftar often begins with dates and water, followed by dishes of spicy vegetables and meats.

⌃ Stalls in Lahore, Pakistan, sell popular Iftar foods such as deep-fried pakoras and samosas.

Pakora
(vegetable fritters)

TIME:
About 1 hour

SERVES:
4 people

TOOLS:
mixing bowl
weighing scales
stirring spoon
grater
knife and cutting
   board
baking sheet
spoon
oven gloves
turner

Vegetarian

Vegan

Dairy Free

Pakoras are a popular, deep-fried, crispy Iftar snack. This is a baked version. Pakoras are fritters made traditionally with chickpea flour (called gram flour or besan), and filled with all sorts of vegetables, such as potatoes, onions and broccoli. If you can't find chickpea flour, you can use plain flour.

INGREDIENTS:
140 g chickpea flour, or plain flour
½ teaspoon salt
½ teaspoon baking powder
½ teaspoon dried cumin
1 teaspoon dried coriander or celery seeds
⅛ teaspoon dried cayenne pepper
125 ml water
1 small potato, peeled and shredded
1 carrot, peeled and shredded
1 small onion, cut into thin strips
non-stick cooking spray

STEPS:

1 Preheat oven to 230°C/ Gas mark 8. In a bowl, mix together the flour, salt, baking powder, cumin, coriander and cayenne pepper. Add the water, a little at a time, stirring after each addition until you have a very thick batter. (You may not have to add all the water.)

Add the shredded potato, shredded carrot and onion. Stir, so that all of the vegetables are coated with the batter.

2

Spray a baking sheet with non-stick spray. Drop the batter in spoonfuls onto the baking sheet. Then spray the tops of the pakoras with non-stick spray.

3

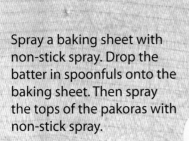

4 Bake for 15–18 minutes. About halfway through cooking, flip over each pakora and press flat so it can brown on both sides.

5 With the turner, transfer them onto a plate and eat them warm from the oven!

The Night of Power

Laylat al-Qadr, the Night of Power, recalls when the Prophet Muhammad heard the first words of the Qur'an from Allah, through an Angel from Allah called Gabriel (in Arabic, "Jibril"). It is the holiest night of the year for Muslims. Traditionally, it is on 27th day of Ramadan.

Sleepless nights

Many Muslims spend all night in prayer. They also recite and study the Qur'an. The day that follows is a public holiday in many Islamic countries, so it does not matter if people stay up all night. In countries like the UK, there may not be a public holiday. Instead, Muslims who own businesses or shops may change their opening times to allow for a sleepless night.

⌃ Muslims gather outside the al-Aqsa mosque in Jerusalem for prayer on Laylat al-Qadr.

Staying up all night

The Qur'an says that the Night of Power is a good night for prayers to be answered. According to Islamic beliefs, a Muslim's past sins are forgiven if the person prays all through the Night of Power.

Muhammad did not give the exact date for the Night of Power, but most experts believe that it was within the last 10 days of Ramadan. For this reason, some stricter Muslims spend all 10 days praying and studying.

Now & Then

Changing priorities

Some Muslims think that Laylat al-Qadr is becoming overshadowed by preparations for festivities. They say that some people don't spend enough time praying. Instead, people shop for clothes, or prepare their homes and food for the feast of Id al-Fitr.

≪ Muslims in Pakistan pray in their mosque, which has been lit for Laylat al-Qadr.

Id al-Fitr – The Feast of Fast Breaking

To mark the end of Ramadan, when the moon rises and a new month begins, Muslims celebrate **Id** al-Fitr.

It's an important holiday time for Muslims, so people go to great lengths to prepare for what is essentially their first midday meal in a month. This is where Muslims "break" or end their fast.

⌃ Children enjoy a ride during the Id al-Fitr festivities in London.

Prayers, lights and food

Early on the first day of Shawwal, Muslims go to the mosque, where the **imam** leads special prayers. They thank Allah for helping them keep the fast.

Afterwards, families gather in their homes, which are often decorated with lights. Greetings cards are exchanged and children are sometimes given sweets, new clothes or money. After a big, traditional midday meal, families might go to concerts, street fairs or the park. In many places, special sporting events also take place, such as camel racing in Saudi Arabia.

Sugar Feast

Id al-Fitr is sometimes called the Sugar Feast or the Sweet Festival. Sweet foods, such as fried syrupy jalebis, are very popular at the midday meal. Spicy foods such as lamb biryani are popular main dishes, with sugary semolina-based puddings to follow.

Charity

Zakah al-Fitr is food that is distributed at the end of the fast of Ramadan. Each individual is meant to donate two handfuls of food, grain or dried fruit to the poor.

⌃ Chinese Muslims gather for a festive lunch at Id al-Fitr.

Baklava

Baklava's nutty filling, flaky pastry and drippy syrup is a sweet treat for Id al-Fitr! It is one of many tasty sweets that Muslims share to celebrate the end of Ramadan. Please see page 44 for more tips on this recipe!

TIME:

About 1½ hours

SERVES:

Makes 8 large squares , or more if you cut them into smaller pieces!

TOOLS:

weighing scales
saucepan
bowl
stirring spoons
30 cm x 20 cm baking
  dish
pastry brush
oven gloves
paper cases

 Vegetarian

INGREDIENTS:

100 ml water
50 g caster sugar (40 g for step 1, plus 1 extra tablespoon approx. 10 g)
50 ml honey
1 teaspoon lemon juice
180 g chopped walnuts
1 teaspoon cinnamon
20 frozen filo sheets (thawed)
150 g butter, melted

STEPS:

1 Heat the water, 40 g of sugar, honey and lemon juice in a saucepan on medium-high heat until it starts to bubble. Reduce the heat to medium-low and simmer for about 10 minutes. Set aside to cool.

2 In a bowl, mix together the walnuts, a tablespoon of sugar and cinnamon.

3 Preheat the oven to 180°C/Gas mark 4. Brush melted butter onto the baking dish. Cut the filo sheets in half. Place one filo sheet onto the bottom of the buttered dish. Brush more butter onto this sheet, and place another one on top. Continue placing and buttering the sheets until you have stacked 15 sheets. Butter the top sheet.

4 Spoon a third of the nut mixture onto the sheets and spread evenly. Then butter and place five more sheets on top. Spoon another third of the nuts, butter and place five more filo sheets. Spoon on the last third of the mixture, and butter and stack the remaining 15 filo sheets. Butter the top layer.

Cut the baklava into squares, all the way through the layers. Bake for about 50 minutes until golden brown.

5

6 Remove from the oven. Pour the cooled syrup into the slits and over the top of the warm baklava.

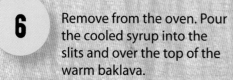

7 Allow to cool. Place each slice into a paper case . Store in the fridge until ready to eat.

CELEBRATING THE HAJJ

Every year, from the 7th to 12th day of Dhu al-Hijjah (the last month of the year), about 2 million Muslims travel to Mecca in Saudi Arabia. They are on a journey called the Hajj. The pilgrimage is the Fifth Pillar of Islam (see page 6). All Muslims who are well and wealthy enough are expected to go on the journey once in their lifetime.

Praying in Mecca

The Ka'bah, or the "cube", is in the Grand Mosque in Mecca. It is the focus of all Muslim prayer. It is believed that the Prophet Abraham was told by Allah to build the **shrine** there.

⌃ Thousands of pilgrims circle the Ka'bah, trying to touch it.

⌃ Pilgrims throw stones at the pillars in Mina because the pillars represent the Devil.

Rites and rituals

On arriving in Mecca, the pilgrims have to obey a list of rules. They sleep outside, carry out rituals and follow a traditional route. On arriving just outside Mecca, the pilgrims bathe, put on special white clothes and pray. Then, they:

- circle the Ka'bah seven times
- sip water from the sacred Zam Zam well
- walk between two hills, Safa and Marwah, seven times
- go to the valley of Arafat to pray and sleep in the open
- **sacrifice** and share a goat or sheep for the end of the pilgrimage feast of Id al-Adha
- gather and later throw 49 to 70 stones at the pillars in Mina over several days
- sacrifice a sheep or goat and then give this meat to the poor
- shave (the men) or cut off a lock of their hair (the women)
- return to the Ka'bah and circle it another seven times
- pray for forgiveness.

Id al-Adha

Id means "festival", and Id al-Adha means "Festival of Sacrifice". This festival and Id al-Fitr are the two most important celebrations for Muslims.

Id al-Adha takes place at the end of the Hajj, on the last day of the year. All around the world, Muslims - even those who have not been on the Hajj that year - celebrate the sacrifice and sharing of animals all around the world, including Muslims who have not been on the Hajj that year. Id al-Adha celebrates the Prophet Abraham's willingness to follow Allah's orders and sacrifice his son.

《 Muslims in Malaysia, cooking a big meal to share for Id al-Adha.

Abraham and Ishmael

During this festival, Muslims remember the story of how Allah asked Abraham to sacrifice his son Ishmael. The Devil tempted Abraham to disobey and so save his son. But Abraham still prepared to do the sacrifice, until Allah stopped him and Allah gave him a sheep to sacrifice instead. Muslims believe Allah was testing Abraham's obedience, and did not really want Ishmael to be killed.

A feast of sacrifice

Id al-Adha is a public holiday in Islamic countries, but all over the world, Muslims go to the mosque to pray at dawn. They visit family and friends, and may exchange gifts.

Some sacrifice a sheep or goat. An animal sacrificed for Id al-Adha has to be of a certain age and of the best quality. The meat then cooked and used in different meals, according to the traditions of the country, such as a biryani in India, or kebabs in Turkey.

In the UK and other non-Islamic countries, the animal has to be killed in a **halal** slaughterhouse. The meat is divided, and family, friends and the poor each get one third.

≫ Lamb kebabs are a popular Id al-Adha meal in Istanbul, Turkey.

FAMILY CELEBRATIONS

At special times during a Muslim's life, there are important events to celebrate and traditions to follow. Some traditions vary from country to country.

Birth of a baby

A new baby is washed, and then the father whispers the Call to Prayer, or Adhan, into the baby's right ear. The father also whispers into the baby's ear the important Muslim beliefs in one God and in the Prophet Muhammad as the messenger of Allah. Some Muslim parents rub honey, sugar or a sweet crushed date onto the baby's gums. It is believed that the sweetness helps the baby drink and digest its milk.

∨ In Indonesia, this baby's grandmother is performing the rituals.

Gifts to the poor

Seven days after the birth, family and friends gather for Aqiqah, a naming ceremony. The baby's hair is shaved and weighed. The same weight of silver is given to the poor, although today most people give money instead. A sheep or goat is traditionally sacrificed, or meat is bought from a shop, and then given to family, friends and the poor.

DID YOU KNOW?

Many Muslims do not celebrate individual birthdays. To celebrate a birthday would be seen as copying a ritual from the non-Islamic world.

⌃ Children learn to recite the Qur'an when they are as young as six.

⌃ Intricate patterns called mehndi are drawn on a bride's hands using a paste made from the leaves of the henna plant.

Changing traditions

Traditionally, Muslim families have tried to find suitable partners for their young men and women to marry. But some young Muslims now find their own husband or wife. Both the bride and groom must agree to the marriage; it is against Islam for them to be forced into marrying each other.

Henna party

In some countries, the bride and her female friends and relatives gather to have fun and sing before the wedding. The bride's hands are decorated with **henna** paste.

Marriage around the world

Muslims may have their wedding ceremony in a mosque, a hall or at home. The style and location of the wedding depends on the country and the families' preferences. However, Muslims all around the world usually wear traditional Islamic wedding clothes.

Before the ceremony, the groom gives the bride a **dowry,** a gift that is hers to keep. The wedding ceremony includes readings from the Qur'an and prayers. An imam or marriage officer leads the ceremony. The bride and groom agree to a wedding contract, called a nikah, in front of witnesses.

A celebration feast called a walimah follows, usually given by the groom's family. Marriages have to be declared publicly and this can be done at the walimah.

♡ An Indonesian couple's wedding. The style of wedding clothes worn by Muslims varies around the world.

CELEBRATIONS AROUND THE WORLD

Muslims celebrate festivals all around the world, often in different ways depending on local traditions. Gatherings for prayers at mosques, readings from the Qur'an, processions and feasts are highlights of Muslim festivals.

>> In Pakistan, a procession to celebrate Milad-un-Nabi', the birthday of Prophet Muhammad, is a mass of green flags.

<< In a mountain village in Bulgaria, Muslims have their own unique wedding traditions, and only marry in winter time. Here, money is attached to the bride's dress.

>> In Indonesia, a procession of bands goes down the streets of Solo (Surakarta) to celebrate Id al-Fitr.

≫ In Malaysia, Muslims celebrate Milad-un-Nabi' with processions, in Melacca City.

≪ In Egypt, a cannon overlooking Cairo is fired during Ramadan to signal sunrise and sunset.

≫ Muslim pilgrims praying in Arafat, Saudi Arabia, during the period of the Hajj pilgrimage.

COOKERY TIPS

Noah's pudding

- To zest orange or lemon peel, clean the outside of the fruit with water. Use a grater with small holes to take off small bits of the fragrant outer peel. Don't grate too deep – the white part is bitter.

Pakora

- Non-stick cooking spray is an easy way to keep your food from sticking to a baking sheet. If you don't have non-stick spray, you can simply rub some vegetable oil on the baking sheet with kitchen roll. Or you can line the sheet with baking paper, found in the baking aisle of most supermarkets.

- Dried spices can lose their smell and flavour if kept too long. The best place to store them is in air-tight containers in a kitchen cupboard. Spices stay freshest in dry, cool places out of sunlight.

- When you add liquid to baking powder, it creates gas bubbles of carbon dioxide. Baking powder helps the dough rise to keep the fritters from becoming dense when baked.

Baklava

- Filo dough is rolled into very thin sheets – as thin as paper! When baked with butter between each layer, they form a rich and flaky pastry. You can find frozen filo dough sheets in the freezer or refrigerated sections of most supermarkets.

TIMELINE

CE

c. 570	Muhammad is born in Mecca
c. 610	Muhammad receives the first words from Allah
c. 622	Muhammad and his followers move from Mecca to Medina
c. 632	Muhammad dies and Abu Bakr is elected as the new Muslim leader, or caliph
c. 655	Islam begins to spread through North Africa
680	Hussein, the Prophet's grandson, dies in battle
732	The Muslim Empire reaches its widest extent
1120	Islam spreads throughout Asia
1918	World War I ends and the last Islamic empire (the Ottoman Empire) ends
1945–60s	Islam spreads further as large numbers of Muslims move to Europe and North America from Asia, Africa and India

GLOSSARY

Abraham Muslims see Abraham as a prophet. Muslims call him Ibrahim.

caliph head or ruler of an Islamic community

dowry something valuable, such as a house or money, brought by a bride to her husband when they get married

fast go without food or drink for a particular period of time

halal food that can be eaten by a Muslim

henna natural red dye that comes from a tree

id (*also spelt* eid) feast

idol image or object, such as a statue, that is worshipped

Iftar evening meal that ends the daytime fast during Ramadan

imam Islamic leader who gives religious guidance and leads worship in the mosque

graven image visual representation of a person, god or animal, that could then be worshipped. This can be a drawing, painting, sculpture or something similar.

Jesus religious leader who is seen as the son of God by Christians and as a prophet by Muslims. Muslims call him Isa.

martyrdom when someone dies or is killed because of his or her religious beliefs

Moses prophet who led his people out of Egyptian slavery. Muslims call him Musa.

pharaoh ruler in ancient Egypt

pilgrimage journey to a holy place that is important to a religion

prophet person who has been chosen to speak for Allah

purify to make clean

ritual religious ceremony or custom

sacrifice offering made to Allah

shrine place that is sacred because of a link to a particular holy person or object

spiritual to do with the spirit or religion rather than the material world

tribe group of people who usually live in the same area and have the same beliefs and culture

FIND OUT MORE

Books
Awesome Qur'an Facts for Kids, Saniyasnain Khan (Goodword Kids, Kindle edition, 2013)
India (Countries Around the World), Ali Brownlie Bojang (Heinemann Library, 2012)
Islamic Culture (Global Cultures), Charlotte Guillain (Heinemann Library, 2012)

Websites
www.bbc.co.uk/schools/religion/islam/index.shtml
Learn more about Islam and its festivals on the BBC website.

www.masjid-umar.org
Listen to live services from the mosque at the Masjid Umar, Leicester.

www.virtualclassroom.org.uk/virtual/newsite/index.htm
Try the quiz on this website, and learn about how Islam and Muslims have contributed to our everyday lives.

Places to visit
Explore Islamic art and objects in the following museums.

British Museum, London
www.britishmuseum.org

Victoria and Albert Museum, London
www.vam.ac.uk

National Museum of Scotland, Edinburgh
www.nms.ac.uk

It is a good idea to contact them in advance to arrange to visit. You should always be quiet and respectful in any place of worship.

Further research
Find more Islamic celebration foods to cook and taste, such as for Id:
www.bbc.co.uk/food/occasions/eid_el-fitr

Find out more about the Hajj:
www.muslimkidsdigest.com/what-is-hajj

47

INDEX

Abraham 5, 20, 34, 36–37
Abu Bakr 11, 45
Adhan 38
Al Hijra 8–9
Alī ibn Abī Tālib 11
Allah (God) 4, 12, 13, 20, 28, 36, 37, 38
aqiqah 39
Arabic 5
Ashura 10, 12–13
ashure 12, 14–15
athletes 24

baklava 32–33, 44
beliefs 4
birth 38
birthdays 16, 39
Bulgaria 42
Buraq 20

caliphs 11
Call to Prayer 25, 38
camel racing 31
charity 6, 22, 31, 35, 37, 39

dates 24, 25, 38
dowries 41

family celebrations 38–41
Farah, Mo 24
fasting 6, 7, 12, 21, 22, 23, 24, 25
Fatima 11
festival calendar 9
festivals 6, 7, 8–33, 36–37
Five Pillars of Islam 6, 34
food, special 12, 18, 31, 37

Gabriel 18, 28
gifts 6, 31, 37
green 19
Gregorian calendar 9

Hadith 5, 6
Hajj 6, 34–35, 36
halal meat 37

henna paste 40
Hijra 8
holy books 5
Hussein 10, 11, 45

Id al-Adha 36–37
Id al-Fitr 7, 29, 30–33, 42, 43
idols 12
iftar 7, 24, 25, 26
imams 31, 41
Indonesia 38, 42
Islam 4–7
Islamic calendar 8, 9

Jerusalem 20, 28
Jesus 5, 20

Ka'bah 34, 35
Kuwait 23

lamps 43
lanterns 22
Laylat al-Miraj 20
Laylat al-Qadr 6, 28–29

Malaysia 43
martyrdom 11
Mawlid an-Nabi 16–19, 42, 43
Mecca 4, 6, 9, 34–35
Medina 4, 8, 9
mehndi 40
Milad-un-Nabi 19
Mina 35
Miraj 20–21
Moses 5, 13, 20
mosques 6, 18, 21, 22, 25, 28, 29, 31, 34, 37, 41
Mount Hira 17
mourning 10, 11
Muhammad, Prophet (pbuh) 4–5, 6, 8, 9, 11, 16, 17, 18, 19, 20–21, 22, 24, 28, 29, 38, 45
Muharram 8–13
music 30
Muslims 4

naat 19
naming ceremonies 38
New Year 8–9
Night of Power 6, 28–29
nikah 41
Noah's ark 12
Noah's pudding 12, 14–15, 44

Pakistan 19, 25, 29, 42
pakora 26–27, 44
Palestine 18, 21
panjut 43
pilgrimages 6, 34–35
prayer 6, 20, 21, 22, 25, 28, 29, 41
public holidays 16, 21, 28, 37
puppetry 23

Qur'an 4, 5, 18, 19, 21, 22, 28, 29, 39, 41

Ramadan 6, 7, 22–29, 43
recipes
    baklava 32–33, 44
    Noah's pudding 14–15, 44
    pakora 26–27, 44
Red Sea 13

sacrifice 35, 36, 37, 39
Shi'a Muslims 10–11, 16
street processions 10, 16, 42, 43
Sugar Feast 31
suhoor 24
Sunni Muslims 10, 11, 12
Sweet Festival 31
sweets 18, 31

Turkey 23, 37

UK 16, 28, 30, 37, 43

vegetable fritters 26, 44

weddings 40–41, 42
worldwide Islam 4
zakah al-Fitr 31